*The Dedalus Press*

*The White Battlefield of Silence*

**James Mc Cabe**

# The White Battlefield of Silence

## JAMES MC CABE

Dublin 1999

The Dedalus Press
24 The Heath
Cypress Downs
Dublin 6W
Ireland

ISBN 1 901233 32 4 (paper)
ISBN 1 901233 33 2 (bound)


Dedalus Press books are represented and distributed in the
U.S.A. and Canada by **Dufour Editions Ltd.**, P.O. Box 7,
Chester Springs, Pennsylvania 19425
and in the UK by **Central Books**, 99 Wallis Road, London
E9 5LN

The Dedalus Press receives financial assistance from
An Chomhairle Ealaíon, The Arts Council, Ireland.

Printed in Dublin by Colour Books Ltd

## Acknowledgements:

The author would like to thank the editors of the follow-ing, where many of these poems first appeared : *Ballymun Echo, The Poetry Ireland Review, The Spectator, Cyphers, Voicefree, Riverine, Cadena, Voices, New Irish Writing* (The Sunday Tribune,) *The Irish Times, Zeitriss* (Augsburg), *The London Magazine, Metre, Stroan, Thumbscrew, New Hiber-nia Review* (Minnesota). Several poems have been broad-cast on *Writer's Bloc* (Dublin Weekend Radio), *Writers Inc.* (Anna Livia FM) and *Rhyme and Reason* (South Dublin Community Radio). Some have won prizes in the Dun Laoghaire/Rathdown Poetry Competition, The Kilkenny Competition and the Clogh Competition. "Fear and Mis-ery in the Third Reich" originally accompanied a perfor-mance of the play of the same name by Pale Mother Theatre Company, in The Crypt Theatre, Dublin, 1996. The author also wishes to acknowledge the assistance of the Arts Council and the Cultural Relations Committee. He wishes to say a special thank you to the Hawthornden Literary Institute, for the opportunity of working in Hawthornden Castle.

# CONTENTS

## I

## II

# III

# IV

I

# Soundings

*In Memoriam Augustine Martin*

The little battalions of words march out
Onto the white battlefield of silence.
Poetry, you said, was like an empire
Surrounded by barbarians, monsters
In the margin. For years like legionnaires
We fought along its cold northern borders.
October like a funeral of leaves
Took you on its shield, our dead emperor,
The wind blowing through our heavy armour,
And the horses of sound on a white field.

## Etymology

*for Drue Heinz*

Every two weeks a language, they say, disappears.
All things flowing, the dictionaries of dead leaves,
The old centuries, vanish like sleeptalk; like some
Snowblind dinosaur drifting among accidents.
Words are ghosts, in whom the past keeps coming alive.

Take English for instance. One of the immortals,
With a Saxon axe, word made flesh made skeleton.
The broken dactyl fingers, the homemade poetry
Only a battlefield, under a Viking sky.
History and language, prisoners of each other.

Which is why we read stories between the storylines,
Under a chainmail rain, the Cyclops' blinded eye.
Words have lives they themselves cannot carry over,
So much semantic luggage, borrowed currency.
Words die and are born. Not one lasts a thousand years.

As if someone, deep in the future, reading this,
Came away defeated, unable to make out
The Gothic fossils and the earthquake vowel shifts
Scribbled in an unknown tongue. The manuscript left
As illegible wreck. Words are Trojan Horses.

But poets, whose job consists of walking back to
Paradise, dream of a Blue and White Nile at the
Confluence of tongues, where the last woolly mammoth
Trapped standing in ice, comes clean in a summer thaw.
Come poet, let us build in the ox-house of the word.

## Memorabilia

*for Katriona*

*See the attic space, is it big enough?*
To hold all the shipwreck of the past.
Silence ambushes here, happens. I am
Overgrown with all I have grown out of.

Sunken with bric-a-brac rubbish-treasure,
The ceiling below is a seabed now —
The cot, and the crib of mummy bundles
Remembered in newspaper for next year.

Big and dead the old radio. Absence
Is the empty ocean of its shell, deaf
To its own dark catch, shoals of sound, voices
Marooned on the cloud of insulation.

Things, it appears, outlive their uselessness.
Like we live their names aloud beached up here
In black: *Stava, Sottens, Vigra, Sundsvaal* . . .
*Bethlehem*, swaddled in the ancient news.

## Percy Place

*for Thomas Kinsella*

The little dead leaves lie at my feet where
The wet black hair of the winter branches
Combs through a white and ghost familiar air.
Ducks and gulls, oblivious to the trash
And boredom of the unemployed canal,
Perform their rituals as if in some
Film, while the traffic like an animal
Snores and moans in the grip of a bad dream.

There is an expectation wherever
Poetry has lived, wherever silence
Like a shell has blossomed into flower.
It's as if, Thomas, the place still listens
Out for you among the siren slaughter,
Motionless, shivering in the water.

## Ascension

*for Máirtín Ó Direáin*

Dying, now your body is dead.
The dead language they tried to keep
Alive is unremembered. Aranman's
Dream stuffed into syllabus, spoonfed
In children's doses, thick vowels
Sticking down our ignorant throats
Compulsory as prayer, the angelus.
We left school and got well, forgot.

Stripped, your poems lie where you left them.
Like old chothes we give to beggars
Who throw them away down the lane,
The clothes no one can wear in our time.
Dreams rise up — a hurry of radio poets
Replacing the advertised programme.

## Coole Park and Ballylee, 1995

Again this place, red rust and autumn gold
Ghosted by morning frost. A cobweb thread
Of light gleams between the railings, a stag
Roars prehistorical in fog, birds flit
Up as the last leaves die, catching the light.

I walk down cold forest corridors, not
Knowing what lifetime, and hear with each foot
The fall of other voices, down to where
A single rock breaks the looking glass
Lake, a whiteness of swans in the distance.

Dark rooks flap beneath the battlements where
A poet built his fortress of words, *Thor*,
And let the world crash in chaos around.
Now as before the flesh will turn to ash,
The griefstricken tree a skeleton dance.

For an instant white hair behind the glass
Stops to look up, sees through me, vanishes.
Pure silence, not a soul about, where I
Fell asleep at the darkening tower,
Woke to shave in the stream's fluent mirror.

**II**

# Watercut

## I — Willow Park Winter

Sky pale as a child's coffin,
A token dimness denoting day.
Snow mauls the garden, driving
Its white tooth into the corners
Or, exhausted from falling, trails
Along branches like gunpowder.
The washing hanging like bones
Shifting with the odd wind.
From an albino skin protrudes
The grassy stubble of two days.

Young willows, winter novices,
Float like dead coral above
An avenue of deserted reef.
The usual lone streetlamp
Presides fanatic on the parade,
Down to their last skin, the
Trees consoled in mutual impotence;
Shrivelled berries tap their
Weighty republics against the
Antlers of paralysed beasts.

Tundra telephone lines bracket
The broken ice-rink park
Trampled to bits early
By some invisible stampede.
The road is meaty slush,
Yet still rejecting colour.
New snow lands on it warily,
Bracing itself fully for
The guttural indigestion
Of a car combing the corner.

In slow motion a begrudging
Planet crawls into view.


## II — Glasnevin Graveyard, The Headstones

Pain does not live here.
It goes and comes with the living
Who bury us, like headaches
On top of collapsed loves.

22

Their chewing eyes dry like
Tongues of lava along these
Paths of fingermarked sky.
And we strip fingerprints
As easily as wet paint.

It's hard to breathe
Where there is no breahting.
Unleavened clouds are broken
And a loaf of rain cathedrals
Down, softening the statues'
Treacle hair. Behind, a fogged
Hothouse in the Botanic Gardens
Shrinks with growth: brainless plants
Styled against a pain-sensitive sky.
I breathe nothing but words,

And choke. Their living
Meaning swallows whole
The wooden roots of this city.
Their memory spelt backwards
Clinging onto our holy boredoms,

Larval in the ground's safe
Freezing womb. Alone and green,
Cherubed with dodos' wings, the
Cartoon of a baby's twin grief.
Just there, I felt the kick

Of their nightmares,
*Our Little Angels.*

## An Orchestra of Rain

The crowd conceives anonymity,
A pavement universe beneath its skin,
A thousand different feet that feel like rain.

Thin stilletto raindrops fall on stone,
Tarmac breathes beneath a bike's rubber lungs,
Dances under the drunken baby's footfalls,

Laps the pawpink pulse of a dog or
Stabs the hydraulic rattling cripple's crutch.
A wheelchair's silent slow waltz makes it think

Of that other invalid the traffic,
Its mutants internally combusted
As for one heavy hour it rains constantly,

Everywhere. Soft splashing of seagull's
Shadows at dusk, the baby falls of a drunk,
As darkness lands again eternally.

No one to watch the dance with the stars,
None to wound its colour with wetness, rain-
Wash the waiting streets where the nightcity walks.

# Masvingo

## I

Stomach launched along the
Rifled runway, our insides climb
From constrictive ground, our
Crowfeet dangling freely.

Suggested into limbless air,
The sky sucking schedule
A cloud-cold Antartic —
No land but a white memory.

London, the channel in an inch,
Broadbacked Europe with its
Languid Danubes, all rush
To Sofia and melting cold.

Sleeping over inland seas
Nightward into Tripoli, a
Spangled necklace carelessly
Flung on the crocodile coast.

A stop to stretch our wings,
The walls clean shaven with
Gadaffis, customs grab a gin-
Happy Infidel, and we watch

Caravans unloading off the tall
Desert, the last straws untied
From coffee camels' broken
Backs — video, hi-fi . . .


## II


Nuclearwide sunrise reacts
On denim horizon, the strict
Azure of wing knifing into
Reddening Tropic of Colour.

Landing on Zimbabwe
In high tide — warm waves
Of chocolate heat lapping
On our close Irish clothes.

Harare on a Sunday —
Not a sinner, one tattered
Tramp shifting like reggae —
Crusoe shipwrecked in urbis.

Masvingo from the air —
Through cake mix propellers
Snakes a muddy river over
Land wild and hairy, gone

Model tiny in a cruel
Parody of silence. From
The red ground — ant armies,
Bridges and the birth of sound.

Froglegged troopcarriers
Burp past. Parked before
A straw scalped mud hut —
One rustfree estate, insisting.

# III

Desert boots dripping into
The floor, the Rover darting
Across flooded bridges, pools
Of heat wetting the road ahead.

Ruins of white farms acne
The post-war bush. A millionaire's —
*The Greatest House in Africa* —
Toppling into the Doric jungle,

Jericho crumbling to silence.
A wildlife park — the lake
That drank itself in drought —
Herds of gnu in the distance —

Thunder-dreamers for the rains.
We turn a corner to confront
The snaking ladder of a giraffe
Aiming its eyes on the

Sitting target of my skin.
A wildcat's cry sounding round
The stones of Great Zimbabwe —
Past citadel of Solomons

And Shebas, or anyone now,
Growing vague in a low fog.
Old capital on an ancient
Sunday — not a sinner.


## IV


Sunset's slashed yolk spilling
Over Silver City's corrugated
Cooking sheets. Twilight —
Shimmering in snowing sunshine.

Drunk, we native into beerhalls.
My flesh like the moonfruit
Bitten into by the black hunger
That fed me full stop in a glass.

Choking toward scalding sickness
Sheets, gashes of lightning
Splitting the hard darkness like
The valium screaming up my veins:

*Jim Ni Kab. Came in*
*Hysterical and dypsomanic*
*Shouting -- thinks he's swallowed*
*A solid in his beer.*

Still choking, a dream strangled
Into my head -- a brother
Naked, atop a roaring jeep
Bellowing *Viva La Papa!*

Into the wide night, rain
Sizzling all our suns now.
Above, the Southern Cross, galaxies
Of silence listening to itself.

Stars stagnate as we hurl
With them through blank space.
*P.S. I enjoyed all the*
*Rough Dublin accents on the phone.*

*Zimbabwe*
*January 1985*

*Zimbabwe*
*January 1985*

## Thunder of the World

Arrow to work in the winter,
The poverty of civil servants
Without mudguards
Cycling lines of muck
In caked construction up their backs.

Thrown from a half shut window,
The butt of a youthful cigarette
Hits ground, lingers its frozen hiatus,
Then crushed and broken,
Flattened by Fords, Volkswagen.

An unhappy woodlouse
Overturned on its back,
The pack of legs
Bleeding in effort
Beneath the muscles of the sun.

The lights of an ambulance
Shoot the iridescent windows
Of a dreary drizzled street.
The words *Forever and Ever Amen*
Spoken from behind you at Mass.

# *Wordables*

## I

I know nothing
And am nothing until
The one who says this

## II

Snapped umbilical
Knotted and sown
The finished word

## III

Imitate life
Then really die

IV

Believe me when I say I cannot go
To church anymore for all my friends
Pray there

V

Ponder the ordinary
Until fear
Electrocutes

VI

Falling in love and going to war
Mona Lisa smiles at the man
In the moon
Drowning in a painted lake

VII

Continents float into each other
Slot together neatly
One pupil island in a wet iris

## VIII

Eve passes the drug
That compensates
For Paradise

## IX

We must wait for promise
And while we wait
There will be no promise
No waiting for promise
Nothing

## X

A tear
Orbits the cheek
To ignite
In the wound
Of the mouth

XI

We have eaten well
Now vomit to taste
Appetite again

XII

Number Seven
Your underclothes
Thrown on the floor
Of my mind

XIII

Children with arms like burnt branches
Reach out on the celluloid

XIV

A fly plucked asunder
By a child's mantis fingers
Insect masses at prayer

## XV

Traitor inherits the prophet
Both inherit a tree

## XVI

Necessity being the mother of illusion
I kissed her with all the loneliness
I had known and was to know

## XVII

Time passes
Burning urine

## XVIII

Each wave
Doubting the shore

## XIX

Strange alone in the womb
Used to the world

## XX

Seconds like wood
Century flashing steel

## XXI

The illiterate swimmer
Drowning down to dream
Once wave again
And disappear

## Lady Dionysus

From here I have dreamt
Your memories to madness.
You crossed the smoke-spiralling
Dance-floor to greet me.
I dreamt you leaving my gate,
Turning a new hairstyle timetable,
Rock-cutting the letters —
*It takes an hour to say hello to you —*

You waited for me outside school,
Drink and freehouses on a Monday.
With glazed eyes you laughed
As you fell off the wall.
I dreamt you quizmaster on a
Country and Western show —
Keeping the peace
With stetson and moustache.

We made a foursome once
And were happy in the
Irresistible attraction of sameness,
Content as four lunatics on Mars.
I dreamt the two of you behind a
Placid field of ripening wheat,
With hair gone long you posed —
Two Gauguins for the passing cider gangs.

You loved me even though
I might crash and
Take to a wheelchair.
I dreamt a military train circling
My bed, stuffed with a single you —
Bandolier-breasted in an armoured truck.
I fall open, gasping, exhausted,
Trusting in the infancy of exile.

## Having Dreamt The Heart

I had a dream the human heart
Was fashioned for lifelong love, it
Dreamt its way through a sickly sleep,
Dream-long and mute behind sound proof
Glass it moved with animal ease.

Nothing of that dream now remains.
The waker is not the one who
Stands inside a sleeping skull,
Only told of his quick offspring
Later, in a faint hunger that
Stares at every sound of breathing.

## *Killiney Beach, Sunday Afternoon*

Turning from the tunnel under the rails,
I ear my way to the hearing waves.

The shore is moving with strangers,
All strange in company and alone
To hear the sea's slow advice.

Bounding a stream that bites the sand
To the bone, my ears fall headlong
Into its pushing brother.

A puppy prances and hops about
The head of an adult Alsatian,
Dogs even finding each other strange . . .

A girlchild chases after a female gang,
Swamped in her mother's anorak.
They stop, and turn, to zip it up.

Turning to the tunnel under the rails,
I ear my way to their swimming graves.

## De Viris Illustribus

Knowing you will not calm down
        Till I am half mad myself,
I concede to you that our life
        Is half worthless and full of
Terror. Nothing left for show,
        We drink, two old waterbuffalo
Scarred at the drinking hour.

And what is it keeps us here:
        Absolute loyalty, of a sort,
Humour, intimacy — the comfort
        And jealousy that springs on
Us. We are locked in a common
        Appetite for language, for
The silences that were women passing.

## Face With Crumbling Edges

*". . .into the sere, the yellow leaf . . ."*
*MacBeth*

I drank to friends — and alcohol
Walks home alone. Lives I left unwinding
Like frayed twine, a frost of stars above
The bloodshot eyes of the trafficlights.
I know. Things take more than a week.

Snail trails, abandoned autographs,
Scrawl into the dark as Dublin Airport
Seduces another soft star to her bed.
Like an ocean the wind listening in
The trees. Know loneliness in a sound.

A hedgehog. Tiptoe forzen as I stoop.
Pass, and it starts up again, a plump
Sod, cut free and shuffling. Nightleaves
Bled white by the lamp leeches, ghostly
Alive over me. In the porch the search for
The key in the unlikeliest pocket,
For the magic word to turn and lock me
Shut into a gethsamene of sleep.
A hedgehog outside wide awake. Rootless,
On a bed of nails, such perfect progress.

The light on in the kitchen. Woken walls.
At the sink send a cold pint of glassy
Water down a throat scorched with thirst.
Turn the tap off. Then three tears. A dry
Drip, the clock all innocence and defeats.

Up the stairs feet guess each step of dark.
A door open on books, paper and bed.
Limp on the desk the resting instruments,
Unless one of them was to think something:
Bloodrush to the pen, erect with intent.
The nib knowing nothing as it knocks
At blankness, a few unsolvable words
To a simple need, and the pen flaccid again.
Above my head a commotion of engine,
A blind night-whale, trawling the darkness.

Hands in a soapy mirror wash my face.
A skeleton fingering the knowledge
That flesh is a kind of debris, and no
One is Narcissus, veins breaking out
In a web, wrinkled in the womb. How

The expressions increase with age, looks
Of sickness coming out of the face
Once a little life is knocked off.
It is the skin of expectations
Peeling, blank blood of tears realising.

The eye itself a face with tears, swollen
In the storm each dreamt hell releases.
If that dream channel will not calm, then
Tie me to a vernacular silence.
The wax in my ears wards off no siren.

## Autumn Treatment

*"No wind no word. Only a leaf,*
*just a leaf and then leaves." Finnegans Wake*

### I

We met as two strangers meet,
In a stranger's dream. I was
Finished work, vague corpse at a bus
Queue, failing to pass the time but
Watch the uprooted wind toss
A black snow of swirling birds.
You were a face I looked at
Before I could recognise — Snake-child,
Hidden for months, coming out of a crowd
The huge weeping sorrow of her hair.

I was twenty with her, and twenty
After her for a little . . .

The heart of the starfish
Does not grow back again.

What we did was without words.
Now we spoke and wasted them,
Not hate in a joke, but to admit
Mutually the difficult truth : both
Speakers without lovers — silence
Like an ivy on the throat.

Leaving me the end of an empty
Queue, quickly taking a bus
Neither you or I would get,
The glass knuckled by thinning trees.
A ten minute walk from the terminus;
Raining slowly, dry leaf sick-falls
Onto the grey stem of the road.
Letting my feet talk in them,
Forgetting the way. Like lemmings
Leaves scurry to the concrete edge.

## II

*Wadelai Park* the bus said
As I was slipping away . . .with
Her chin beside me once, she really
Sat, legs of leaves in her tights.

Pinewood dream, drink on me . . .

When your face was the sudden
Of my heart, stone knot of tongue.

A girlish house, long stranded hairs
Monsooning the sofa. My beard
On your breast, learning the quiet there.
Gypsy-legged in skin-warm feet,
My jumper around you as your furs.
Sitting up, then pouring hair
I tasted your lick in my ear
(Yours, a rose of flesh, so lovely . . .)

Regretting what is said and not said
In a wise, ignorant silence.

The seats of the cinema stood erect
In the shuttered dark where debauched yellow
Lamps sunken into the ceiling mooned
Immortal over us, cracking the hard
Boiled sweets of our skulls in the blue.
All but the first love is too late.

Twice watched, the film assumes with
A polished moon, false tan running
Under a gossiping Irish sky
Tripping up a kerb, then 'kiss me!'

    Your face swimming like wine
    In my papercup eyes

Words on water were floating seeds, then
Were sudden stone sunk by the Tolka.
Trees flame up darker than the night,
Their souls sleeping in the water,
Fleshed with the hearts of false love
Where voices wake in the downriver
Lovered dark. The cold nippling her.

    Our words kisses and our quiet
    Which of us stopped each kiss

We are not a river, friend, and though
Two lovers are the whole world
We cannot become one water, our faces
Rivered together as if there were no

Dreams to keep from each other, our
Heart's bark carved with the last lost
Love. And all the world we were
Until the pools in our eyes held no colour
And we walked through them, as two strangers met
Heading for distant roads of the dream.

Birds beginning to perch
On the silences of our telephone

A little longer the last minute leaves

Before words happen again
Like little crumpled silences
Your mind precise and changed
As a crowd of pigeons
Of one mind take off

Making a crowd of the one absence.
I close my ears and feel an empty
Embrace abolish me. A rose
On its own fought the darkness outside.

Too late, memory hands back our
First week — meeting for the bus like mad.
Shaving awfully, full of hotblooded
Shyness, each morning found me beside
That wounded tree — its black tarred scar,
Your name a tongue on every bird.
Days when I wrote smooth, without error,
No matter what thinking tried on them,
Words in escape, not stopping. Only once
A strand of you fell from my arm.

### III

The last month of autumn a new coldness;
A drowned worm at the bottom of a rain puddle

Loneliness stuck the jumper you wore to my back.
Friends smelling a wound, a noticeable
Limp in conversation, and the table
Of empty pints moving in with friendly
Determined interrogation. Outnumbered,
On a diet of cigarettes and rain
In solitary rooms of hours eating
With disgust, avoiding certain songs

On the radio . . . and the heart
Does not grow back, leaves only a black
Spot somewhere in some notebook to let
It be known and lost. A vellous rain
Strewn with the corpses of leaves to kill
Time being. But honest past could not die,
The leaf of your tongue would hold
For as long as it believed in you — when I
Remembered the last, tongueless kiss;
Our one hometruth a deeper lie.

## Sunspots

*In Memoriam Dermot Lea*

*¿Ay cuantas veces eres la que el odio no nombra?* — *Neruda*

### I

Afternoon, the confused quiet of a library.
A navy tall figure walking towards
The biography of infinity and that was all
I saw. The longitudes of your going
As silent as dust blown from a cover,
A title made from a few last words
Stared at forever. Most of my life
Happened in that minute. Now I
Learn to read what the shadows say, to
Live each day as one who leaves the world.

### II

As you did before rain began one night
To redden the windscreen. Thrown twelve
Feet from inflammable future, the point
Blank kiss of headlights hundreds of heavens
An hour when elastic darkness finally
Snapped and the sun invaded your eye.

Its body became your destination :
Success losing each battle to embrace
A bastard transplant, every wound
A metal eye for the untouched end.

### III

The first time I ever saw words
*With beaded bubbles winking at the brim*
You in a class reciting the consumptive.
His hand holding the glass you held
As the syllable wine was spoken that
Sung to the surface and swam free.
Me gulping the quicksand of a female
Daydream, woken only by words gleaming
Like sunlight as far from a drowning
Fist as stars are from the night.

### IV

Night turns to the blind, the blind
To themselves. And for a long time now I
Have been mising your words with mine,
They spawn strange children — all unknown

Jungled darknesses chasing, only memory's
Acid rain to guess them across the one
Rope bridge dangling its slashed sentence
Into the abyss, my page. Bird-black blindness
Slicing a white silence, and on it
Your guessing death as good as mine.

## V

Tonight a coffin is my planet.
(Woodworm already at the wood in my
Dead eyes.) A solar candle drinks the wax
Of orbit about you — coral chrysalis
In solid shroud — your future will close
Like an eyelid when all that I see will be
A bubble sun wobble up a glass sky,
Leaving this earth and our thirst to watch
Us take leave of each other — astronauts
Exploding off the edges, like sunspots.

III

## Among Cloud

*for Bernadette*

Among cloud, the engine alone among
The dream of itself, we sit it out while
The world does not move. We have crossed the Alps
And the mountains of the moon, the white caves
Of God's pockets, the flock of all our souls,
White tiger of my solitude moving.

Travel light, forget the flame and the smile,
Fill the empty grave of the suitcase,
Take it to the heart's lonely trainstation,
Hurry — like tadpole rain wriggles across
The window (your own lunatic shadow) —
And be a drunken currach in the dark.

Until you land in a fog of druid oak,
Beached from the voyage of your sleep.
All our past is the magic music from
An ice-cream van, buried in winter now.
You I recognise in the first blind look,
The fallen giant silk parachute of snow.

# Death of Adam

*. . . the snake-seed free,*
*and the fled garden*
*fills with knowledge . . .*

The first winter who keeps us
Wil find two spit pips for his
Snowman's eyes to feel the fruit
And feet of human gravity.
Conversations will seem like
Something I almost forgot to bring.

Which you know isn't like me,
But having words to play with
Isn't the same anymore.
Mention the leaves and whirls
Of the hour left me — flakesoft
Whispers to hush
                    our stereo fall.

Outside, the sugarbowl snow
Is an unknown woman.
Tomorrow her shroud will lift
From the face of the bloody grass,
And morning will stir
A broken rib of loneliness.

# First Christians

## I

The waves of her veil captured
Like the waves on the pier — sepia
Sea-breeze stands to attention
Behind the communicant posing
For camera, a waiting icecream
Melting around her hands.

## II

Skin grew with it from the start,
Wrapping the raging furnace in
White paper. The flat earthed host
Stamped on her tongue, her mouth
A catacomb of quiet to receive
Amounts of death only the flattest
Host could carry. Fed on hunger,
Tasting awkwardly its blood and bread,
She quenches her heart with prayer:
To give to Caesar the other cheek
Cheerfully lacerated on its platter.
Can there be a wine for those
Who had lost all water at Cana?

# III

To know nothing. And secrets.
To know not the hour — a roaring
Cortina careers through the old woman
Straight after church like a soft-bellied
Bag of rubbish — religion
Drying off her clothes like seaweed.

## Willow Park Revisited

In dreams I find myself at the back wall
Staring up at the big blue beautiful
Sky of summer, leaves washing in the wind
Like underwater. Calm, blue, eternal.

In dreams I lie out in the back garden
In some summer out of the Seventies,
And watch the peace that holds in little things
Like the daisy stem bending with the bee.

In dreams the sky is full of contraptions,
Zeppelin and bi-plane, airship, insect,
Blackbird and sparrow, magpie, crow, seagull.
A butterfly angel hovers in white.

In my dream I swim back to Willow Park,
Float over hedges and walls, to see how
The garden is golden in the late sun
And wake to find all the world lost in snow.

# Clare Island Revisited

Heading west, the road curls up to where trees
Branch out and embrace themselves, until whale
Shapes at last float out through the ancient mist:
Clew Bay, all Tír na nÓg in smithereens.

Heading west, the boat rolls in a slate grey
Sea until the mainland is lost in thought
And the island comes close like a live dream,
Cut like a key to complete the jigsaw.

Heading west, the road turns to grass until
Nothing but pure cliff and sheer sky is left.
Lazybed ribs are the bones of a poem
Where famine lost its voice and became ghost.

Your crooked teeth tore Armada's belly
And swallowed *El Gran Grin* like a stone, then
You closed your lips on the foreign tongue, *brón*
*Na dtonnta as seo amach agus riamh.* *

* *Sadness of the waves from now on and before*

# *Cliara Haiku*

## *I - XXX*

# I

Follow these green steps
Into the sea, this story
From another world . . .

# II

My island survey —
Childhood dream and memory
In the whale's belly.

# III

Roonagh, rust and rope,
Bearded seaweed walls, old chains
Dancing in the swell.

# IV

Clew Bay like a school
Of dolphins, with Clare Island
Like a humpbacked whale.

# V

*The Dolphin* crossing,
Parachutes of jellyfish
Billow beneath us.

## VI

Gaelic *Cliara*,
Like a beautiful woman
Seen once in real life.

## VII

Celtic Otherworld —
Avalon, Atlantis, Tír
Na n-Óg — your pen-names.

## VIII

At one time a part
Of mainland Europe — for miles
Offshore drowned forests.

## IX

Listen carefully —
You can hear a thousand ghosts
All speaking Gaelic.

## X

Days after her death,
My ten year old grandmother
In a photograph.

# XI

With all my heart I
Hear the heartbroken, carefree
Cry of the curlew.

# XII

Cliara abbey —
Littered with the dead, the ground
Itself looks like waves.

# XIII

My greatgrandfather
Buried somewhere here, sleeping
Beside Granuaile.

# XIV

The O'Malley plaque —
*Terra et mare potens* —
Cold black skull and bones.

# XV

This crumbling fresco —
But still clear a yellow man
Arrowed in the back.

## XVI

Portnakilly, where
I plunged into the ice-womb,
Mother Atlantic.

## XVII

Beetlehead, somewhere
Out there the lost bones of a
Broken Armada.

## XVIII

Dead crabs on the shore,
Desert, old broken armour,
Ancient crusaders.

## XIX

From this cliff look down
At the massive Atlantic
Like living marble.

## XX

Cloudless summer sky —
All except for a single
Chalk scar, vanishing . . .

## XXI

Knockmore, cloud shadow
Racing in silently from
The west, the New World.

## XXII

Like an odyssey
Of islands — Turk, Bofin and
All Connemara.

## XXIII

Bill's Rocks, where the birds
Are tame to the touch, unknown
To humanity.

## XXIV

Holidays — like a
Past or an afterlife — no
Mainland memory.

## XXV

The sweeping beam of
The old lighthouse a thing of
The past, a dreamt dream.

## XXVI

Out into the pitch
Darkness invisible . . . but
Stars in their millions.

## XXVII

Lassau, little wood,
Island oasis in this
Brown desert of bog.

## XXVIII

Elephant's graveyard :
Stumps and tusks of ancient pine,
Unforgettable . . .

## XXIX

Clare Island autumn —
The leaves of long vanished trees
Fall in their millions.

## XXX

*Nostos*, or journey
Home, only this nostalgia
Is like homelessness.

*Propaganda*

*A Poem in Progress*

## Thermopylae: A Dream

Not the film of history this
Time but the real dream of itself:
A sword flashing and falling through
The altogether different sky
Between the mountains and the sea.

Into your hand, Leonidas
The Real, battered, blasted, betrayed
On all sides, for three days against
The impossible multitude,
The rich difference of a dream.

Elsewhere your life is happening
As you watch the golden soldiers
Wither in a rain of arrows
Who combed their long hair at the Hot
Gates, who will not wake at Sparta.

## Fear and Misery in the Third Reich
*after Brecht*

### The Faithful

Here come the Brownshirts
Under a swastika sky —
Polished, shaven, like
Boyscouts, but for the jackboots,
But for the odd beer belly.

### Pageant

Rome in its glory
Cannot compare with this, our
City floating with
Red flags, flowers on the streets,
Our women dressed for weddings.

### The Jewish Wife

Somebody shoud have
Told him a Jew was no good
For a wife, that they
Nearly always disappeared,
That gentlemen prefer blondes.

*Parenthood*

One Fatherland, one Leader,
The little children learn to
Look at their parents
In a new light — good, or bad
Germans, as the case may be.

*Somnambulist*

Like a sleepwalker
The Führer arrives, gloves in
Hand, he knows there is
Nothing to wake for,
When dreams come true.

*Hitler's Hands*

Like little tyrants
They wag an index finger
To call the lackey
Over, or fold in a bored
And impatient *Heil Hitler*.

*In the Art Gallery*

Connoisseurs of art,
They follow their Leader through
The naked statues
Who have studied the human
Form in all its perfection.

*The People*

What the people need
Is blood and iron, not bread
And circuses. Give
Them guns instead of butter,
A full stomach comes later.

*The Economy*

Foreign debts? Don't pay
Them. Unemployment? Put them
To work building roads.
Then fill them with the People's
Car — *Panzerkampfwagen.*

*Charity*

God is with us
At Christmas, Santa Claus from door
To door, the party
Men with their bundles of rags
The rich have no more time for.

So Hermann Goering
With his Teddybear smile, is
Taking time out from
The Final Solution to
Spread a little happiness.

*The Facts*

History is what
The Party believe in, what
Every Nazi in the street
Knows to be true — all
The rest is propaganda.

## Mandate

The next election
Will be a simple affair;
Every man and woman will
Repeat after me the words:
*Gott mit uns, Adolf Hitler.*

## Settlement

This is without doubt
Our last territorial
Claim — all those lands where
Germans live or have lived or
Want to live in the future.

## Lebensraum

In a dream I woke —
Another place, other time —
Everyone was gone
Except for huge black ravens
The bloom of health, sleek, well-fed.

81

*Clean Streets*

These are the days, when
Crime is a thing of the past,
When you wouldn't see
A scrap of litter, even
The cobblestones are scrubbed clean.

*A Critic*

There is no such thing
As fear or misery in
Our Third Reich, Herr Brecht,
That is exactly what we
Intend to eradicate.

*New Order*

I see the future —
A bright, empty autobahn,
A string of dirty
Red cattle trucks heading
In the opposite direction.

## Anschluss

Now the beggar has become Emperor,
Takes in his hand the spear of destiny,
The millennial blood of history;
Takes, at last, command of the pure future.

Let us say something in the nature of
Satisfaction brings a smile to that face
Where once was penniless and grey disgrace;
King of Vienna, not its obscure slave.

Now for two thousand days the world will burn,
And flesh no longer come soft to the touch
Till the cold panzer jaws of this Reich reach
The longest river, the highest mountain.

Christ dies again, nailed to a crooked cross
And crowds along the Ringstrasse hail the new
Tiberius. Tonight there is no snow,
The air is cold, the stars like shattered glass.

## Blitzkrieg Tanka


*Thit duilleog agus*
*Duilleog eile mar an spéir*
*Féin ag fáil bháis, nuair*
*A tháinig é faoi dheireadh —*
*Amhrán troda an dhomhain.* *


### Polen


Upsidedown in air
The legs of frozen horses
Stiff as sculpture where
The sky swallows a distant
Scream of the crooked eagle.


### Frankenreich


Like an empty shell
A lost bugle in the sand
Where the shield-wall broke:
An old hollow conch through which
The sea speaks: *Peace in our time* . . .

## Griecenland

Go tell the Spartans
Leonidas died in vain.
Now through the Hot Gates
Persians are pouring again,
In a fleet this time of steel.

## Kreta

Not the island now
Of sunburnt Icarus who
Like a feather fell,
But the sky alive with noise
And snowing with paratroops.

*Leaf after leaf fell,*
*Like the sky itself*
*Was dying,*
*When it came at long last —*
*The war-song of the world.*

85

# Panzer

Like something prehistoric now
That once roamed in great herds over
Sand and steppe, a last grey panzer
Threatens the dead museum air.
One by one, a carcass of thirst
Or frozen in the big snows, they
Vanished, left you here to trumpet
Your extinct, Pyrrhic victories.

## Oradour-Sur-Glane

*On Saturday 10th June 1944, the village of Oradour-Sur-Glane
in France was surrounded by soldiers of the Waffen-SS. Over six
hundred inhabitants were massacred and the village left a
burning wreck. No definite cause for the action has ever been
found.*

And then one afternoon late in the war
History arrived in trucks. Instead of
First Holy Communion the schoolchildren
Taken out and promised sweets, photographs.
Instead of shopping and the tobacco
Ration, the village suddenly strange with
The foreign voices and the camouflage.
Instead of the afterdinner coffee
Hotel guests told to assemble quickly
Outside with the others — covered with flour,
The baker stripped to the waist; the half-shaved;
The sick schoolteacher in her dressing gown;
The friend on a visit, unable to
Trust the calm assurance of the mayor,
Not knowing the novelty of terror
One Saturday afternoon in summer.
Again and again in his copybook
A boy had written out in punishment
The sentence: *Je prends la résolution
De ne jamais faire de mal aux autres.*

87

Unburied, the warm ochre of your bones
Grows long shadows in the late evening sun.
Altar and bath are open to the sky,
The doctor's car a holocaust of rust
And birds alone to watch the falling leaf.
Still the river is a mirror for its
Trees as they replace the leaves of each year,
But here in this archaelogy of
Empty streets the tramlines and telegraph
Poles are waiting for Godot. Here silence
Is a souvenir, a sweing-machine
Left on a window sill until nothing
But the pure idea of things is left:
The penknife and the watch, the wedding ring,
The cigarette case punctured with a hole,
The extinct clock that stopped, and then started
Counting the minutes of eternity,
The pale flush of leaves in a summer breeze,
The slow snow falling from a blindfold sky,
*De ne jamais faire de mal aux autres.*

One by one and years later the guilty
Die, surrounded by friends and family,
From natural causes. Unless they too
Were slaughtered in the aftermath — battle
Massacre where no coward could find hope.

But for the one who lived it merely meant
Getting on with things, forgetting the war,
The black and white photographs, moving back
Into the colour film of his real life.
Except, possibly, once in a while when
A dream sweats him awake, back there again:
*'Today you're going to see the blood flow.'*
Six hundred in a single afternoon,
And not a loss to show for it, but for
The single accidental casualty,
Dropping down dead under a falling brick.
They too were human after all, given
The last, tragic irony — some of them
Alsatian and Frenchmen like yourselves,
*De ne jamais faire de mal aux autres.*

The faces smile in the photographs that
Tell each grave apart, children looking to
The future, all innocence unconscious,
Out of the unimaginable past:
Of bicycles along green summer lanes,
Of polka dot trout flashing in the Glane,
Of birthdays, the fluttering butterfly,
The tram's familiar, friendly hum before
The caterpillar squeal of a halftrack.
The rest unidentified, buried as

One flesh, except for two glass coffins where
The charred, indiscriminate bones of some
Offer themselves for display; other ones
Discovered at the bottom of a well,
Or shop escaping halfway through a fence,
The infant found in the baker's oven,
The old man left for dead in his own blood,
Or hurriedly buried in shallow graves,
One blind hand reaching up through the garden,
*De ne jamais faire de mal aux autres.*

In the church the women and children wait,
As their men are led into garages
And barns. No one knows how long it will take,
The officer pauses for translation,
Something about terrorists, that was it,
One afternoon at a quarter past two,
The war at an end, the ordeal over,
Clouds clearing after the morning drizzle.
At half past three the church bell, then stutter
Of a machine gun as the killing starts,
The furious agreement of small arms
Before the last, diligent pistol shots,
The crackle of sparks, the dark cloud, the sound
Of a German voice on the gramophone.
Days later at the burnt-out church a man

Comes across his wife holding her mother,
Both bodies at a touch disintegrate,
The little churchbells melted in the heat,
The bullet-riddled pram at the altar,
*De ne jamais faire de mal aux autres.*

*Nevermore to harm others*, a promise
That was easily kept. Nows clouds like ghosts
Throughthe smuuer move, and all possible
Harm cannot again disturb the sudden
Permanence of this place. Oradour, lost
Ocean inside the shell, the syllables
Of your name can never translate into
The beautiful excuse of poetry,
But only an empty hush of leaves where
Tramtracks rust in the cobblestone silence,
Suddenly ancient as Thira or lost
Atlantis, swallowed in the avalanche.
The fire-black bicycle hangs on a wall,
Unused to such capricious idleness,
And wooden shutters shipwreck in the sun.
In a dream's aerial photography
I flew over your honeycomb ruin,
Village of a thousand whispers, from which
History now has departed for good,
Leaving you with all the time in the world.

## *Orpheus in Auschwitz*

When Orpheus, great hero, came
To play before the King of Hell
For the shade of Eurydice
Still nursing her wounded ankle,
Not one in all the Underworld —
Rolling boulders or breaking rocks —
Not one looked up or forgot, while
The trees and stones stood where they were.

## An Angel Surveys
## the Ruins of Dresden

In your hand you seem to hold
All the rubble of Europe,
As if you had waited for
This one chance to come alive,
Or offer something maybe
To the skeleton city
By way of flesh or nurture.

From the City Hall you watched
The labyrinth fill with flame,
But could not move your black robes
Or turn your face away from
The indescribable rose
That gathered all its fury
On the dark stem of the Elbe.

They are burning the dead, heaped
Like leaves, unidentified,
Who dreamt about the future
As if the war were over,
Before the black bombers came
And pulled a blanket of flame
Across the sleeping city.

Dresden angel, how could you know
When the sirens screamed all clear
That this was not the end?
That more would share your salt tears
In the terrible desert,
Your stone and frozen sorrow,
*Mar aingeli gan Dia . . .**

[*"*Like angels without a God . . .*"]

## Eagle's Nest

Our little corporal has left Olympus,
The island Alp above the world, and gone
Underground the god, at least, of his own
Bunker, berserk in the shirt of Nessus.

His world shrinks in a magnifying glass
Who held the future with an eagle's eye,
And dreams again the wet trench, the greasy
Backstreet, lost in a cloud of coloured gas . . .

*In the window it was always summer,*
*The sugarbowl snow, the silver tray lake.*
*Tyrants in the afternoon almost took*
*Leave of their nature, ate cake, took pictures.*

But this is more recent : Berchtesgaden
Broken under a blue sky, blank ashes,
And absent the hosts of such emptiness --
Adolf, Eva, burning in the garden.

*April 1945*

95

## A Visit to Kinsella

An afternoon of high skies, luminous
With cloud, shadow-shouldering mountainsides.
Follow the valley up to where a gash
Of waterfall silk tells you he would live —
All silence, forest, eagle ancient air.
Upstairs the massive desk, the books shipshape
Under bright skylight shields, a telescope
Aiming at invisible daylight stars.
All this happened already, or before,
When you sat and felt the pure commitment
Like an old fog-bound Viking, reaching for
The uncertainties. Then for a moment
Silence held like poetry between us,
And then sudden rain, like endless applause.